THE UNEXPLAINED

THE
LOCH NESS
MONSTER

BY DAVID SCHACH

BELLWETHER MEDIA · MINNEAPOLIS, MN

Are you ready to take it to the extreme?
Torque books thrust you into the action-packed world
of sports, vehicles, mystery, and adventure. These books
may include dirt, smoke, fire, and dangerous stunts.
WARNING: read at your own risk.

Library of Congress Cataloging-in-Publication Data

Schach, David.
 The Loch Ness monster / by David Schach.
   p. cm. -- (Torque : the unexplained)
 Summary: "Engaging images accompany information about the Loch Ness Monster.
The combination of high-interest subject matter and light text is intended for students in
grades 3 through 7"--Provided by publisher.
 Includes bibliographical references and index.
 ISBN 978-1-60014-502-5 (hardcover : alk. paper)
 1. Loch Ness monster--Juvenile literature. I. Title.
 QL89.2.L6S33 2010
 001.944--dc22   2010008478

This edition first published in 2011 by Bellwether Media, Inc.

Printed in the United States of America, North Mankato, MN.

080110   1162

CONTENTS

CHAPTER 1
SOMETHING IN THE WATER

In April of 1960, Tim Dinsdale went to Scotland. He had heard stories of a creature lurking in the lake called Loch Ness. Dinsdale was determined to find **evidence** of the legendary Loch Ness Monster.

Dinsdale searched with binoculars and talked with local people. After five days, he hadn't seen a thing. He was almost ready to give up his search. He would spend one more day looking for the monster.

Photography experts in the British Armed Forces examined Dinsdale's film. They concluded that the film was no hoax. The object in the water, they said, was at least 16 feet (5 meters) long, 6 feet (1.8 meters) wide, and 5 feet (1.5 meters) high.

Dinsdale was driving alongside Loch Ness that morning. He noticed a long, oval shape moving in the water. Dinsdale quickly pulled over and grabbed his video camera. For four minutes, he filmed the shape moving back and forth. Then the shape disappeared beneath the waves.

What did Dinsdale catch on film? Was it the Loch Ness Monster, or was it a **hoax**? No one knew for sure.

Tim Dinsdale

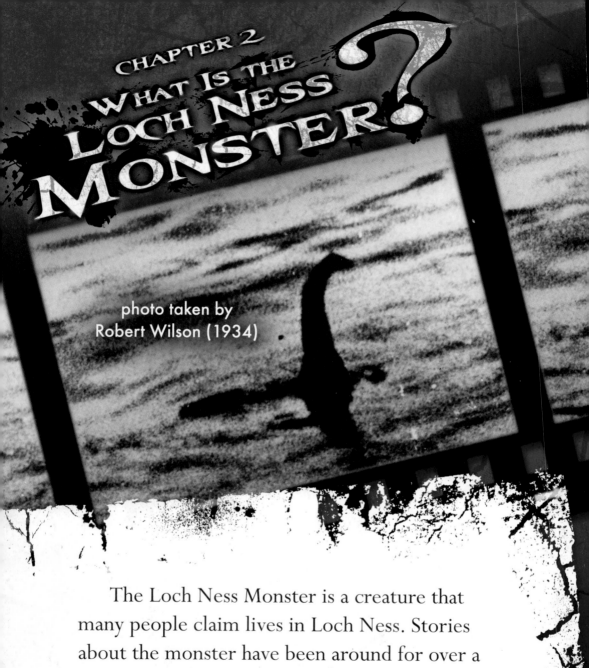

CHAPTER 2

WHAT IS THE LOCH NESS MONSTER?

photo taken by Robert Wilson (1934)

The Loch Ness Monster is a creature that many people claim lives in Loch Ness. Stories about the monster have been around for over a thousand years. No one has ever provided clear evidence of the monster's existence. However, many people have tried to take photographs of the monster. Some of the photos appear to be genuine, but others appear to be fake.

photo taken by
Anthony Shiels (1977)

Do these photos prove
the Loch Ness Monster exists,
or are they hoaxes?

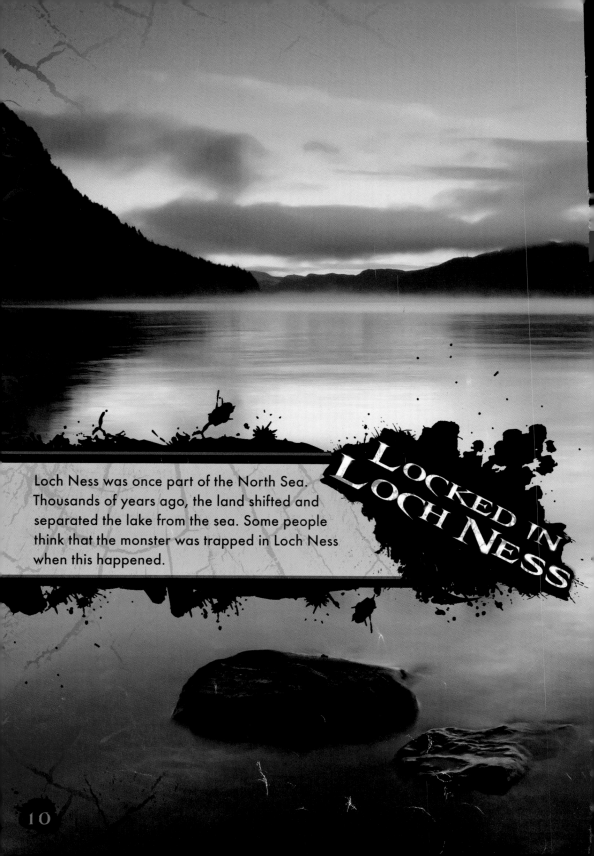

Loch Ness was once part of the North Sea. Thousands of years ago, the land shifted and separated the lake from the sea. Some people think that the monster was trapped in Loch Ness when this happened.

LOCKED IN LOCH NESS

Loch Ness is a large lake. It is 24 miles (39 kilometers) long and 1 mile (1.6 kilometers) wide. Some parts of the lake are more than 800 feet (244 meters) deep. The water is very cold. **Silt** makes the water dark. These traits make it possible that a monster could be hiding in the lake.

HISTORY OF THE MYSTERY

Year
567

1880

1930

1933

1934

1960

1963

1996

2003

2007

Event

Irish monk Saint Columba reports seeing a sea monster attack a man in Loch Ness.

Duncan McDonald sees a creature while examining a sunken boat in Loch Ness.

Three fishermen see a large creature swimming toward their boat.

Many sightings are reported, including the first photograph of the monster by Hugh Gray.

Physician Robert Wilson takes the most famous photograph of the monster; the photograph is later proven to be fake.

Tim Dinsdale captures a four-minute film of a large object moving along the surface of Loch Ness.

A group of farmers sees a giant beast rise above the surface of Loch Ness, then dive back beneath the water.

Local resident Gary Campbell sees a large black hump rising above the surface of Loch Ness.

The British Broadcasting Corporation launches a huge search for the monster, but no evidence of it is found.

Gordon Holmes captures a video of a black object moving quickly across the surface of Loch Ness.

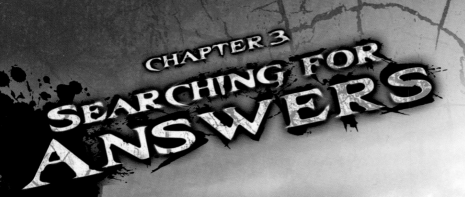

CHAPTER 3
SEARCHING FOR ANSWERS

Dan Taylor used this yellow submarine to look for the Loch Ness Monster in 1969.

underwater camera

Does the Loch Ness Monster exist? Dozens of people have investigated Loch Ness to try to answer this question. Searchers have set up cameras around the lake. **Submarines** have looked below the lake's surface.

The best evidence anyone has found comes from **sonar** imagery. Sonar has shown large objects beneath the lake's surface. The sonar images could just be large fish, but many people think they are proof of the monster.

sonar

NESSITERAS RHOMBOPTERYX

In 1975, British naturalist Peter Scott gave the Loch Ness Monster the scientific name *Nessiteras rhombopteryx*. The name is Greek for "the Ness monster with the diamond-shaped fin."

plesiosaur

If the monster does exist, what is it? Some think it is a whale, dolphin, or giant squid. The most popular **theory** is that the monster is a **plesiosaur**. This giant water reptile is believed to be **extinct**. Some people argue that a small number of plesiosaurs could have survived in Loch Ness. The lake's many fish would provide the creatures with food.

coelacanth

BACK FROM THE DEAD

Scientists once believed that a huge fish called the coelacanth was extinct. However, in 1938, the fish was found off the coast of Africa. Could the plesiosaur be the next creature to surprise scientists?

The debate about the monster isn't likely to end soon. It is difficult to prove either that the monster exists or that it is a hoax. If it does exist, the deep, dark waters of Loch Ness will likely hide it forever.

GLOSSARY

evidence—physical proof of something

extinct—no longer living

hoax—an attempt to trick people into believing something

plesiosaur—an ancient water reptile believed to be extinct

silt—fine particles of dirt

sonar—machinery that uses sound waves to detect objects underwater

submarines—vessels that can travel underwater

theory—an idea that tries to explain why something exists or happens

TO LEARN MORE

AT THE LIBRARY

DeMolay, Jack. *The Loch Ness Monster: Scotland's Mystery Beast*. New York, N.Y.: Rosen Publishing, 2007.

Flaherty, A.W. *The Luck of the Loch Ness Monster: A Tale of Picky Eating*. Boston, Mass.: Houghton Mifflin, 2007.

Wallace, Holly. *The Mystery of the Loch Ness Monster*. Chicago, Ill.: Heinemann Library, 2006.

ON THE WEB

Learning more about the Loch Ness Monster is as easy as 1, 2, 3.

1. Go to www.factsurfer.com.

2. Enter "Loch Ness Monster" into the search box.

3. Click the "Surf" button and you will see a list of related Web sites.

With factsurfer.com, finding more information is just a click away.

INDEX

The images in this book are reproduced through the courtesy of: Andreas Meyer, front cover, pp. 16-17; Dariusz Gora, pp. 4-5; Peter King/Getty Images, p. 5 (small); Ian Tyas/Getty Images, pp. 6-7; Fortean Picture Library, pp. 7 (small), 9; Popperfoto/Getty Images, p. 8; Francois Loubser, pp. 10-11; Ralf Juergen Kraft, pp. 12-13; Fortean/Topham/The Image Works, pp. 14-15, 15 (small); NOAA/Science Photo Library, p. 16 (small); Dorling Kindersley/Getty Images, pp. 18-19; Peter Scoones/Getty Images, p. 20 (small); Christian Darkin/Photo Researchers, Inc., pp. 20-21.